★ THE ★
UNITED
STATES
PRESIDENTS

WILLIAM H.
HARRISON

Heidi M.D. Elston

**Checkerboard
Library**

An Imprint of Abdo Publishing
abdobooks.com

★ ★ ★

ABDOBOOKS.COM

Published by Abdo Publishing, a division of ABDO, PO Box 398166, Minneapolis, Minnesota 55439. Copyright © 2021 by Abdo Consulting Group, Inc. International copyrights reserved in all countries. No part of this book may be reproduced in any form without written permission from the publisher. Checkerboard Library™ is a trademark and logo of Abdo Publishing.

Printed in the United States of America, North Mankato, Minnesota
052020
092020

THIS BOOK CONTAINS
RECYCLED MATERIALS

Design: Emily O'Malley, Kelly Doudna, Mighty Media, Inc.
Production: Mighty Media, Inc.
Editor: Jessica Rusick

Cover Photograph: Alamy
Interior Photographs: After Gilbert Stuart/Getty Images, p. 16; Albert de Bruijn/iStockphoto, p. 37; AP Images, p. 36; Bob Pardue/Alamy, p. 19; George Peter Alexander Healy/Getty Images, p. 20; Getty Images, pp. 5, 29; Library of Congress, pp. 6 (Anna Harrison), 7, 15, 18, 26, 30, 31, 33, 40; North Wind Picture Archives, pp. 6, 12, 13, 17, 21, 27; P&P/Library of Congress, p. 23; Pete Souza/Flickr, p. 44; Philip Gendreau/Getty Images, p. 11; Shutterstock Images, pp. 38, 39; Stock Montage/Getty Images, p. 25; Wikimedia Commons, pp. 14, 22, 40 (Washington), 42

Library of Congress Control Number: 2019956485

Publisher's Cataloging-in-Publication Data
Names: Elston, Heidi M.D., author.
Title: William H. Harrison / by Heidi M.D. Elston
Description: Minneapolis, Minnesota : Abdo Publishing, 2021 | Series: The United States presidents | Includes online resources and index.
Identifiers: ISBN 9781532193545 (lib. bdg.) | ISBN 9781098212186 (ebook)
Subjects: LCSH: Harrison, William Henry, 1773-1841--Juvenile literature. | Presidents--Biography--Juvenile literature. | Presidents--United States--History--Juvenile literature. | Legislators--United States--Biography--Juvenile literature. | Politics and government--Biography--Juvenile literature.
Classification: DDC 973.58092--dc23

★ CONTENTS ★

William H. Harrison

William H. Harrison was the ninth president of the United States. He served as president for just one month. This is the shortest time spent in office by any US president.

Before becoming president, Harrison served in the US Army for many years. He rose in rank to major general. Harrison also worked in farming and tried his hand at business. After the **War of 1812**, Harrison served in both houses of Congress. He also served in the Ohio state senate.

Harrison began his presidential term on March 4, 1841. At his **inauguration**, he gave a long speech in cold, rainy weather. Harrison caught a cold. He died one month later from **pneumonia**. Harrison was the first president to die in office.

As president, Harrison did not have time to accomplish great things. But as a military leader, Harrison played an important role in American history.

TIMELINE

1794

On August 20, Harrison fought at the Battle of Fallen Timbers.

1811

Harrison won the Battle of Tippecanoe.

1798

Harrison resigned from the military. President John Adams appointed Harrison secretary of the Northwest Territory.

1773

On February 9, William Henry Harrison was born in Charles City County, Virginia.

1791

Harrison joined the military as an ensign in the First Regiment of Infantry.

1813

Harrison fought victoriously in the Battle of the Thames.

1800

President Adams made Harrison governor of the Indiana Territory.

1795

Harrison married Anna Symmes.

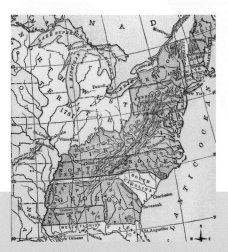

1814

Once again, Harrison resigned from the military.

1819

Harrison was elected an Ohio state senator.

1828

President John Quincy Adams made Harrison minister to Colombia.

1841

On March 4, Harrison became the ninth US president. William H. Harrison died on April 4.

1816

Harrison won election to the US House of Representatives.

1825

Harrison won election to the US Senate.

1836

Harrison lost the election for president to Martin Van Buren.

> **"** Sound morals, religious liberty, and a just sense of religious responsibility are essentially connected with **all true and lasting happiness."**

WILLIAM H. HARRISON

DID YOU KNOW?

★ William H. Harrison was the last US president to be born under British rule.

★ At 67, Harrison was the oldest man to be elected president in the 1800s.

★ Harrison was the first Whig president.

★ Harrison is the first president whose grandson later became president. His grandson Benjamin Harrison became the twenty-third US president in 1889.

★ Harrison was the only president who studied to be a medical doctor.

★ Anna Harrison gave birth to the most children of any First Lady.

Early Years

William Henry Harrison was born on February 9, 1773, in Charles City County, Virginia. At the time, Virginia was a British colony.

William was the youngest of seven children. He had four sisters and two brothers. William's parents were Benjamin Harrison and Elizabeth Bassett Harrison. The Harrisons were wealthy and well-known. They lived on a plantation named Berkeley on the James River.

Benjamin, William's father, was the governor of Virginia. He was called "the Signer" because he had signed the **Declaration of Independence**.

William studied at home until 1787. He later went to Hampden-Sydney College in Virginia. There, he studied classics and history. In 1790, William decided to become a doctor. So, he left college and moved to Philadelphia, Pennsylvania. There, he studied medicine.

FAST FACTS

BORN: February 9, 1773

WIFE: Anna Symmes (1775–1864)

CHILDREN: 10

POLITICAL PARTY: Whig

AGE AT INAUGURATION: 68

YEAR SERVED: 1841

VICE PRESIDENT: John Tyler

DIED: April 4, 1841, age 68

**The Berkeley plantation,
William's childhood home**

In 1791, Benjamin Harrison died. William was sad because he had been close to his father. By law, most of Benjamin's money and land went to his oldest sons. As the third son, William did not get as much money. Now, he had to get a job. So, he left his medical studies.

The Frontier

On August 16, 1791, Harrison joined the military. President George Washington appointed him an **ensign** in the First **Regiment** of **Infantry**. Harrison was young, but he was determined. He gathered 80 men. Together, they headed into the western wilderness of the United States. There, they would fight Native Americans for land.

Today, the site of the Battle of Fallen Timbers is a state park. It is located near Toledo, Ohio.

Harrison marched his men over the Allegheny Mountains to Fort Pitt in Pittsburgh, Pennsylvania. Then, they took boats down the Ohio River. They landed at Fort Washington in Cincinnati, Ohio. This area was called the Northwest Territory. It became home to Harrison for most of his life.

Harrison learned all he could about the military. He soon earned respect for his bravery. On August 20, 1794, Harrison fought at the Battle of Fallen Timbers. There, the US Army defeated Native Americans.

The Battle of Fallen Timbers ended fighting in the Northwest Territory. It also led to the Treaty of Greenville, which was signed on August 3, 1795. In it, Native Americans gave up claims to most of present-day Ohio. They also transferred parts of today's Michigan, Illinois, and Indiana to the United States. That same year, Harrison rose to the rank of commander. He took command of Fort Washington.

The Miami people were living in parts of the Northwest Territory. Miami chief Little Turtle signed the Treaty of Greenville.

Family and Career

While at Fort Washington in 1795, Harrison met Anna Symmes. Anna had been born in New Jersey and was well educated. Harrison and Anna married that November.

Judge John C. Symmes

Anna's father, Judge John C. Symmes, did not approve of the marriage at first. He felt Harrison's military career was too unstable to support a family. And, he knew his daughter would have to endure the hardships of frontier life. Yet Harrison eventually won over Judge Symmes.

The Harrisons had a long, happy marriage. They had six sons and four daughters. The family never had a lot of money. But they were close and loving.

In 1797, Harrison became an army captain. He resigned the following year. Then, he and his family settled on a farm at North Bend, Ohio. They lived in a four-room log cabin. Over the years, Harrison added 12 more rooms to their home.

The Harrison family liked to have people over to their home. Harrison invited many friends, travelers, and politicians for dinner. It cost a lot of money to feed the large Harrison family and their guests. Sometimes, they went through a whole ham in one day!

Anna Harrison

In 1798, President John Adams made Harrison secretary of the Northwest Territory. The following year, Harrison became the territory's first delegate to the US Congress. In Congress, he worked hard for the American people. Harrison's ideas were well-liked.

Harrison pushed Congress to pass the Land Act of 1800. This law changed the way land was sold. Before, land was sold in huge **tracts**. So, only rich people could afford it. The Land Act split land into smaller sections. It became easier for poor settlers to buy land.

President John Adams

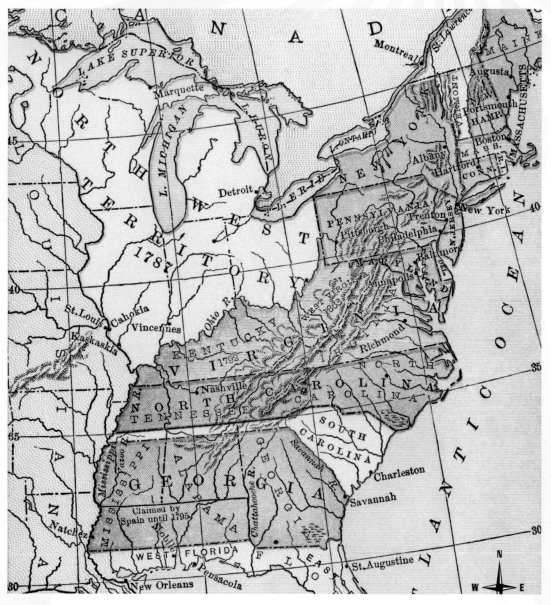

Congress passed the Northwest Ordinance on July 13, 1787. This law provided for the government of the Northwest Territory. This region eventually became Ohio, Indiana, Illinois, Michigan, and Wisconsin. It also included part of Minnesota east of the Mississippi River.

Governor Harrison

In 1800, the Northwest Territory was divided into the Ohio and Indiana Territories. President Adams named Harrison the first governor of the Indiana Territory. Harrison served as governor for 12 years.

Governor Harrison

Governor Harrison tried to improve the well-being of the local Native Americans. He barred alcohol sales to them. And, he ordered their **inoculation** against **smallpox**.

But Harrison's main job as governor was to get land for settlers. As governor, Harrison made several treaties with Native Americans to gain their land. These treaties were often unfair to Native Americans. Harrison gained many acres of land in Indiana and Illinois for settlement.

While serving as governor of the Indiana Territory, Harrison and his family lived in present-day Vincennes, Indiana. Their home is called Grouseland and is open for tours.

Many Native Americans were upset about losing their land. So, they joined together under Shawnee Native American chief Tecumseh and his brother, known as the Prophet. In 1811, Harrison led American troops into battle. They defeated the Native Americans at Tippecanoe River near Lafayette, Indiana. The victory earned Harrison the nickname "Old Tippecanoe."

For a while, the Battle of Tippecanoe stopped problems between Native Americans and settlers. But by 1812, Native Americans were again attacking settlements.

Meanwhile, Harrison began fighting in the **War of 1812**.

President James Madison made him a brigadier general. In 1813, Harrison was promoted to major general.

Later that year, Harrison recaptured Detroit from the British. On October 5, he won the Battle of the Thames. This battle took place on the Thames River in Ontario, Canada. There, Harrison's troops defeated the British and their Native American **allies**. With this important victory, Harrison secured America's northwestern border.

President James Madison

US forces greatly outnumbered the British and Native American forces at the Battle of the Thames.

Working for His Country

In 1814, Harrison once again quit the military. He returned to his farm in North Bend. Besides farming, Harrison tried his luck in other businesses. But each failed.

Harrison still wanted to work for his country. He was popular in Ohio. So, many people encouraged him to run for Congress. In 1816, Harrison won election to the US House of Representatives. He served as a representative until 1819. That year, Harrison was elected an Ohio state senator. He held this position until 1821.

John Quincy Adams

In 1825, Harrison was elected to the US Senate. He was a senator until 1828. That year, President John Quincy Adams made Harrison minister to Colombia. However, Andrew Jackson became president the next year. He sent a new minister to replace Harrison.

Harrison gained valuable political experience during his time as a representative, a state senator, and a US senator.

Bid for President

Many people thought Harrison could become president. He had a strong record in the military. He also had a good record in Congress.

In 1836, the **Whig** Party nominated Harrison to run for president. However, the party was divided. So, it also nominated Daniel Webster and Hugh L. White. The **Democrats** nominated Martin Van Buren.

Harrison faced off against Webster, White, and Van Buren. Harrison's supporters believed he could unite the party. He did well in the election. But he did not earn enough votes to win. Van Buren won the presidency with 170 electoral votes.

Shortly after President Van Buren began his term, the Panic of 1837 struck. The nation suffered an economic depression. Businesses closed, and many people lost their jobs. The nation suffered greatly. As a result, many Americans grew unhappy with President Van Buren. The depression affected his chances for reelection.

President Martin Van Buren

Tippecanoe and Tyler Too

The year 1840 brought another presidential election. Times were hard in the United States. Many people remained out of work. The North and the South argued about slavery. Most people blamed the problems on President Van Buren.

A poster for an 1840 William H. Harrison rally

Once again, the **Whig** Party nominated Harrison to run for president. Harrison chose John Tyler as his **running mate**. Tyler was a former senator from Virginia. The Whigs believed Tyler would help gain support in the South.

President Van Buren was Harrison's opponent. Harrison believed he could beat Van Buren in this election. He campaigned hard and gave many speeches.

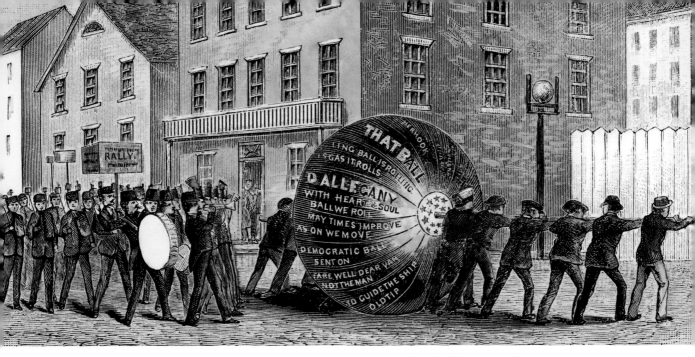

A group of Whig supporters pushed a ball covered
in Harrison advertising for hundreds of miles. This
started the common phrase, "Keep the ball rolling!"

Harrison's campaign was like a traveling carnival. He
had floats in parades. He gave away hats and other items to
gain voter support. Voters were reminded that Harrison was
a military hero. His **slogan** "Tippecanoe and Tyler Too!"
was heard around the country.

A record number of people voted in the election.
Harrison won the presidency! He received 234 electoral
votes to Van Buren's 60. Tyler was named Harrison's vice
president.

The Ninth President

In 1841, Harrison set out from Ohio for Washington, DC. Mrs. Harrison was too sick to travel. Jane Irwin Harrison, Harrison's daughter-in-law, went with him. She would act as White House hostess during Harrison's time in office.

On March 4, 1841, Harrison was **inaugurated** as the ninth president of the United States. It was a windy, cold, and rainy day. President Harrison gave one of the longest inaugural speeches ever. He stood in the cold without a hat or a coat.

President Harrison was worn out from his long campaign and went to bed that night with a bad cold. Later that month, the cold developed into **pneumonia**. William H. Harrison died on April 4, 1841. It was a sad day for his wife, children, friends, and fellow Americans. Mrs. Harrison never made it to Washington, DC. She was preparing to leave Ohio when she received the sad news that her husband had died.

The US government was in a tough position. At the time, the US **Constitution** said the vice president should take on the president's duties. But it did not say if the vice

President Harrison's inauguration took place on the East Portico of the US Capitol.

president should become president or if a new presidential election should be held. The United States had not been faced with this issue before. So, Vice President Tyler named himself president.

During his short time in office, President Harrison had named his **cabinet**. However, Tyler disagreed with Harrison's cabinet members on many issues. Tyler was a former **Democrat**. He still believed in many of the Democratic Party's ideas. President Tyler **vetoed** many **Whig**-supported bills. So, all the cabinet members except **Secretary of State** Daniel Webster quit.

Harrison served the shortest presidency in American history. People believe he could have been a great president. William H. Harrison remains one of the nation's respected military leaders.

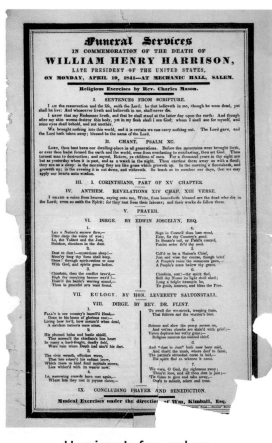

Harrison's funeral was held in Washington, DC.

John Tyler served the remainder of Harrison's term.
He lost his bid for the presidency in 1844.

PRESIDENT HARRISON'S CABINET

ONE TERM
March 4, 1841–April 4, 1841

- ★ **STATE:** Daniel Webster
- ★ **TREASURY:** Thomas Ewing
- ★ **WAR:** John Bell
- ★ **NAVY:** George Edmund Badger
- ★ **ATTORNEY GENERAL:** John Jordan Crittenden

President William H. Harrison

OFFICE OF

BRANCHES OF GOVERNMENT

The US government is divided into three branches. They are the executive, legislative, and judicial branches. This division is called a separation of powers. Each branch has some power over the others. This is called a system of checks and balances.

★ EXECUTIVE BRANCH

The executive branch enforces laws. It is made up of the president, the vice president, and the president's cabinet. The president represents the United States around the world. He or she oversees relations with other countries and signs treaties. The president signs bills into law and appoints officials and federal judges. He or she also leads the military and manages government workers.

★ LEGISLATIVE BRANCH

The legislative branch makes laws, maintains the military, and regulates trade. It also has the power to declare war. This branch consists of the Senate and the House of Representatives. Together, these two houses make up Congress. Each state has two senators. A state's population determines the number of representatives it has.

★ JUDICIAL BRANCH

The judicial branch interprets laws. It consists of district courts, courts of appeals, and the Supreme Court. District courts try cases. If a person disagrees with a trial's outcome, he or she may appeal. If a court of appeals supports the ruling, a person may appeal to the Supreme Court. The Supreme Court also makes sure that laws follow the US Constitution.

THE PRESIDENT

★ QUALIFICATIONS FOR OFFICE

To be president, a person must meet three requirements. A candidate must be at least 35 years old and a natural-born US citizen. He or she must also have lived in the United States for at least 14 years.

★ ELECTORAL COLLEGE

The US presidential election is an indirect election. Voters from each state choose electors to represent them in the Electoral College. The number of electors from each state is based on the state's population. Each elector has one electoral vote. Electors are pledged to cast their vote for the candidate who receives the highest number of popular votes in their state. A candidate must receive the majority of Electoral College votes to win.

★ TERM OF OFFICE

Each president may be elected to two four-year terms. Sometimes, a president may only be elected once. This happens if he or she served more than two years of the previous president's term.

The presidential election is held on the Tuesday after the first Monday in November. The president is sworn in on January 20 of the following year. At that time, he or she takes the oath of office:

> *I do solemnly swear (or affirm) that I will faithfully execute the office of President of the United States, and will to the best of my ability, preserve, protect and defend the Constitution of the United States.*

LINE OF SUCCESSION

The Presidential Succession Act of 1947 defines who becomes president if the president cannot serve. The vice president is first in the line of succession. Next are the Speaker of the House and the President Pro Tempore of the Senate. If none of these individuals is able to serve, the office falls to the president's cabinet members. They would take office in the order in which each department was created:

Secretary of State

Secretary of the Treasury

Secretary of Defense

Attorney General

Secretary of the Interior

Secretary of Agriculture

Secretary of Commerce

Secretary of Labor

Secretary of Health and Human Services

Secretary of Housing and Urban Development

Secretary of Transportation

Secretary of Energy

Secretary of Education

Secretary of Veterans Affairs

Secretary of Homeland Security

While in office, the president receives a salary of $400,000 each year. He or she lives in the White House and has 24-hour Secret Service protection.

The president may travel on a Boeing 747 jet called Air Force One. The airplane can accommodate 76 passengers. It has kitchens, a dining room, sleeping areas, and a conference room. It also has fully equipped offices with the latest communications systems. Air Force One can fly halfway around the world before needing to refuel. It can even refuel in flight!

Air Force One

If the president wishes to travel by car, he or she uses Cadillac One. It has been modified with heavy armor and communications systems. The president takes

Cadillac One

Cadillac One along when visiting other countries if secure transportation will be needed.

The president also travels on a helicopter called Marine One. Like the presidential car, Marine One accompanies the president when traveling abroad if necessary.

Sometimes, the president needs to get away and relax with family and friends. Camp David is the official presidential retreat. It is located in the cool, wooded mountains of Maryland. The US Navy maintains the retreat, and the US Marine Corps keeps it secure. The camp offers swimming, tennis, golf, and hiking.

When the president leaves office, he or she receives lifetime Secret Service protection. He or she also receives a yearly pension of $207,800 and funding for office space, supplies, and staff.

Marine One

George Washington

Abraham Lincoln

Theodore Roosevelt

	PRESIDENT	PARTY	TOOK OFFICE
1	George Washington	None	April 30, 1789
2	John Adams	Federalist	March 4, 1797
3	Thomas Jefferson	Democratic-Republican	March 4, 1801
4	James Madison	Democratic-Republican	March 4, 1809
5	James Monroe	Democratic-Republican	March 4, 1817
6	John Quincy Adams	Democratic-Republican	March 4, 1825
7	Andrew Jackson	Democrat	March 4, 1829
8	Martin Van Buren	Democrat	March 4, 1837
9	William H. Harrison	Whig	March 4, 1841
10	John Tyler	Whig	April 6, 1841
11	James K. Polk	Democrat	March 4, 1845
12	Zachary Taylor	Whig	March 5, 1849
13	Millard Fillmore	Whig	July 10, 1850
14	Franklin Pierce	Democrat	March 4, 1853
15	James Buchanan	Democrat	March 4, 1857
16	Abraham Lincoln	Republican	March 4, 1861
17	Andrew Johnson	Democrat	April 15, 1865
18	Ulysses S. Grant	Republican	March 4, 1869
19	Rutherford B. Hayes	Republican	March 3, 1877

THEIR TERMS

LEFT OFFICE	TERMS SERVED	VICE PRESIDENT
March 4, 1797	Two	John Adams
March 4, 1801	One	Thomas Jefferson
March 4, 1809	Two	Aaron Burr, George Clinton
March 4, 1817	Two	George Clinton, Elbridge Gerry
March 4, 1825	Two	Daniel D. Tompkins
March 4, 1829	One	John C. Calhoun
March 4, 1837	Two	John C. Calhoun, Martin Van Buren
March 4, 1841	One	Richard M. Johnson
April 4, 1841	Died During First Term	John Tyler
March 4, 1845	Completed Harrison's Term	Office Vacant
March 4, 1849	One	George M. Dallas
July 9, 1850	Died During First Term	Millard Fillmore
March 4, 1853	Completed Taylor's Term	Office Vacant
March 4, 1857	One	William R.D. King
March 4, 1861	One	John C. Breckinridge
April 15, 1865	Served One Term, Died During Second Term	Hannibal Hamlin, Andrew Johnson
March 4, 1869	Completed Lincoln's Second Term	Office Vacant
March 4, 1877	Two	Schuyler Colfax, Henry Wilson
March 4, 1881	One	William A. Wheeler

Franklin D. Roosevelt

John F. Kennedy

Ronald Reagan

	PRESIDENT	PARTY	TOOK OFFICE
20	James A. Garfield	Republican	March 4, 1881
21	Chester Arthur	Republican	September 20, 1881
22	Grover Cleveland	Democrat	March 4, 1885
23	Benjamin Harrison	Republican	March 4, 1889
24	Grover Cleveland	Democrat	March 4, 1893
25	William McKinley	Republican	March 4, 1897
26	Theodore Roosevelt	Republican	September 14, 1901
27	William Taft	Republican	March 4, 1909
28	Woodrow Wilson	Democrat	March 4, 1913
29	Warren G. Harding	Republican	March 4, 1921
30	Calvin Coolidge	Republican	August 3, 1923
31	Herbert Hoover	Republican	March 4, 1929
32	Franklin D. Roosevelt	Democrat	March 4, 1933
33	Harry S. Truman	Democrat	April 12, 1945
34	Dwight D. Eisenhower	Republican	January 20, 1953
35	John F. Kennedy	Democrat	January 20, 1961

LEFT OFFICE	TERMS SERVED	VICE PRESIDENT
September 19, 1881	Died During First Term	Chester Arthur
March 4, 1885	Completed Garfield's Term	Office Vacant
March 4, 1889	One	Thomas A. Hendricks
March 4, 1893	One	Levi P. Morton
March 4, 1897	One	Adlai E. Stevenson
September 14, 1901	Served One Term, Died During Second Term	Garret A. Hobart, Theodore Roosevelt
March 4, 1909	Completed McKinley's Second Term, Served One Term	Office Vacant, Charles Fairbanks
March 4, 1913	One	James S. Sherman
March 4, 1921	Two	Thomas R. Marshall
August 2, 1923	Died During First Term	Calvin Coolidge
March 4, 1929	Completed Harding's Term, Served One Term	Office Vacant, Charles Dawes
March 4, 1933	One	Charles Curtis
April 12, 1945	Served Three Terms, Died During Fourth Term	John Nance Garner, Henry A. Wallace, Harry S. Truman
January 20, 1953	Completed Roosevelt's Fourth Term, Served One Term	Office Vacant, Alben Barkley
January 20, 1961	Two	Richard Nixon
November 22, 1963	Died During First Term	Lyndon B. Johnson

PRESIDENT		PARTY	TOOK OFFICE
36	Lyndon B. Johnson	Democrat	November 22, 1963
37	Richard Nixon	Republican	January 20, 1969
38	Gerald Ford	Republican	August 9, 1974
39	Jimmy Carter	Democrat	January 20, 1977
40	Ronald Reagan	Republican	January 20, 1981
41	George H.W. Bush	Republican	January 20, 1989
42	Bill Clinton	Democrat	January 20, 1993
43	George W. Bush	Republican	January 20, 2001
44	Barack Obama	Democrat	January 20, 2009
45	Donald Trump	Republican	January 20, 2017

Barack Obama

PRESIDENTS MATH GAME

Have fun with this presidents math game! First, study the list above and memorize each president's name and number. Then, use math to figure out which president completes each equation below.

1. Bill Clinton − William H. Harrison = ?

2. William H. Harrison + Herbert Hoover = ?

3. William McKinley − William H. Harrison = ?

Answers: 1. Harry S. Truman (42 − 9 = 33)
2. Ronald Reagan (9 + 31 = 40)
3. Abraham Lincoln (25 − 9 = 16)

LEFT OFFICE	TERMS SERVED	VICE PRESIDENT
January 20, 1969	Completed Kennedy's Term, Served One Term	Office Vacant, Hubert H. Humphrey
August 9, 1974	Completed First Term, Resigned During Second Term	Spiro T. Agnew, Gerald Ford
January 20, 1977	Completed Nixon's Second Term	Nelson A. Rockefeller
January 20, 1981	One	Walter Mondale
January 20, 1989	Two	George H.W. Bush
January 20, 1993	One	Dan Quayle
January 20, 2001	Two	Al Gore
January 20, 2009	Two	Dick Cheney
January 20, 2017	Two	Joe Biden
		Mike Pence

WRITE TO THE PRESIDENT

You may write to the president at:

The White House
1600 Pennsylvania Avenue NW
Washington, DC 20500

You may email the president at:

www.whitehouse.gov/contact

★ GLOSSARY ★

ally—a person, a group, or a nation united with another for some special purpose.

cabinet—a group of advisers chosen by the president to lead government departments.

Constitution—the laws that govern the United States.

Declaration of Independence—an essay written at the Second Continental Congress in 1776, announcing the separation of the American colonies from England.

Democrat—a member of the Democratic political party. When William H. Harrison was president, Democrats supported farmers and landowners.

ensign (EHNT-suhn)—an infantry officer of what was formerly the lowest commissioned rank.

inaugurate (ih-NAW-gyuh-rayt)—to swear into a political office. Something relating to being inaugurated is inaugural. A ceremony in which a person is sworn into office is an inauguration.

infantry—soldiers trained and organized to fight on foot.

inoculation—the process of giving a person or an animal a preparation made from killed or weakened germs or viruses to prevent disease.

pneumonia (nu-MOH-nyuh)—a disease that affects the lungs and may cause fever, coughing, or difficulty breathing.

regiment—a large military unit made up of troops.

running mate—a candidate running for a lower-rank position on an election ticket, especially the candidate for vice president.

secretary of state—a member of the president's cabinet who handles relations with other countries.

slogan—a word or a phrase used to express a position, a stand, or a goal.

smallpox—a contagious disease marked by a fever and blisters on the skin. The blisters often leave permanent scars shaped like little pits.

tract—an area of land.

veto—the right of one member of a decision-making group to stop an action by the group. In the US government, the president can veto bills passed by Congress. But Congress can override the president's veto if two-thirds of its members vote to do so.

War of 1812—from 1812 to 1815. A war fought between the United States and Great Britain over shipping rights and the capture of US soldiers.

Whig—a member of a political party that was very strong in the early 1800s but ended in the 1850s. Whigs supported laws that helped business.

ONLINE RESOURCES

Booklinks
NONFICTION NETWORK
FREE! ONLINE NONFICTION RESOURCES

To learn more about William H. Harrison, please visit **abdobooklinks.com** or scan this QR code. These links are routinely monitored and updated to provide the most current information available.

★ INDEX ★